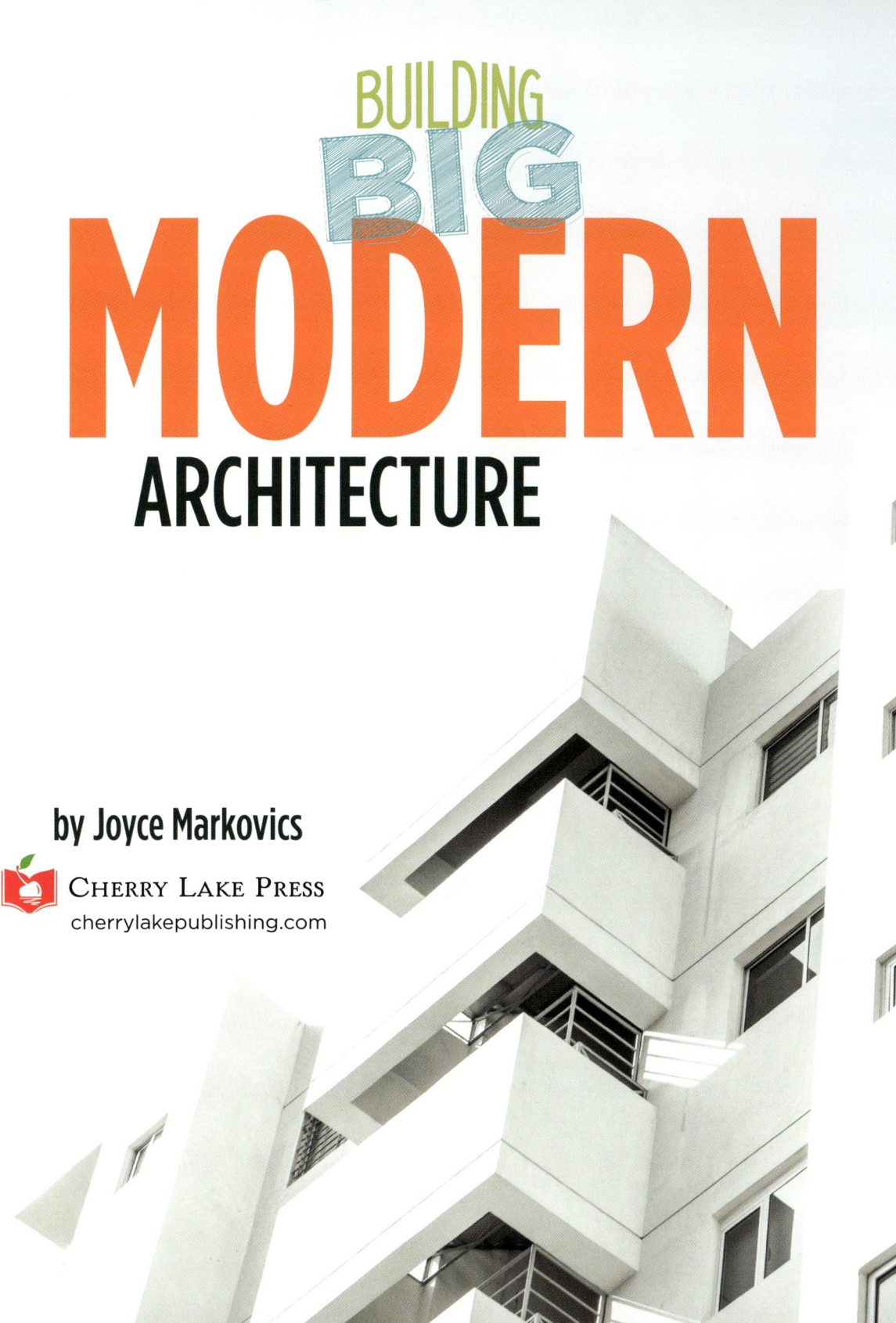

BUILDING BIG MODERN ARCHITECTURE

by Joyce Markovics

CHERRY LAKE PRESS
cherrylakepublishing.com

Published in the United States of America by Cherry Lake Publishing Group
Ann Arbor, Michigan
www.cherrylakepublishing.com

Reading Adviser: Beth Walker Gambro, MS, Ed., Reading Consultant, Yorkville, IL
Content Adviser: Jeffrey Shumaker, AICP, Urban Designer, Planner, Architect, and Educator
Book Designer: Ed Morgan

Photo Credits: freepik.com, cover; freepik.com, title page; flickr/Lenny K Photography, 4-5; Wikimedia Commons, 6; © Barry Peake/Shutterstock, 7; freepik.com, 8-9; freepik.com, 10-11; freepik.com, 12; Wikimedia Commons/New York World-Telegram and the Sun staff photographer: Al Ravenna, 13; unsplash.com/Jim Witkowski, 14; unsplash.com/Joel Filipe, 15; Library of Congress/Highsmith, Carol M, 16; unsplash.com/Kirk Thornton, 17; Library of Congress/Highsmith, Carol M, 18; Wikimedia Commons/Stevenuccia, 19; © Science History Images/Alamy Stock Photo, 20; flickr/m-louis, 21; Wikimedia Commons/Deutsche Bundespost Berlin, 22; Wikimedia Commons/Victor Grigas, 23; Library of Congress/ Highsmith, Carol M, 24 top; Wikimedia Commons/Edelteil, 24 bottom; Wikimedia Commons/Ken OHYAMA Berlin, 25; freepik.com, 26-27.

Copyright © 2023 by Cherry Lake Publishing Group
All rights reserved. No part of this book may be reproduced or utilized in any form or by any means without written permission from the publisher.

Cherry Lake Press is an imprint of Cherry Lake Publishing Group.

Library of Congress Cataloging-in-Publication Data

Names: Markovics, Joyce L., author.
Title: Modern architecture / by Joyce Markovics.
Description: Ann Arbor, Michigan : Cherry Lake Publishing, [2023] | Series:
  Building big : amazing architecture | Includes bibliographical
  references and index. | Audience: Grades 4-6
Identifiers: LCCN 2022039570 (print) | LCCN 2022039571 (ebook) | ISBN
  9781668919859 (hardcover) | ISBN 9781668920879 (paperback) | ISBN
  9781668923535 (adobe pdf) | ISBN 9781668922200 (ebook) | ISBN
  9781668924860 (kindle edition) | ISBN 9781668926192 (epub)
Subjects: LCSH: Modern movement (Architecture)—Juvenile literature.
Classification: LCC NA682.M63 M36 2023 (print) | LCC NA682.M63 (ebook) |
  DDC 724/.6—dc23/eng/20220824
LC record available at https://lccn.loc.gov/2022039570
LC ebook record available at https://lccn.loc.gov/2022039571

Printed in the United States of America
Corporate Graphics

CONTENTS

"A Perfect Building" 4
What Is Modern Architecture? 10
Building Modern. 14
Other Key Examples 22
After Modernism 26

Design a Modern Building. 28
Glossary. 30
Read More 31
Learn More Online 31
Index 32
About the Author. 32

"A Perfect Building"

In New South Wales, Australia, there's a building that juts into the sky like towering ship sails. It's made from glass and giant, curved slices of white concrete that look like interlocking seashells. The Sydney Opera House is one of the most famous—and unforgettable—**modern** buildings in the world.

Danish architect Jørn Utzon designed the Sydney Opera House in 1957. Utzon was inspired by ancient **temples** in South America. He was also influenced by nature, including the image of a bird opening its wings. Utzon wanted to build a "perfect building" that was so beautiful "it is called poetry." Utzon later said, "I like to be on the edge of the possible."

The Sydney Opera House rises 213 feet (65 meters) into the air. It's home to a performing arts center.

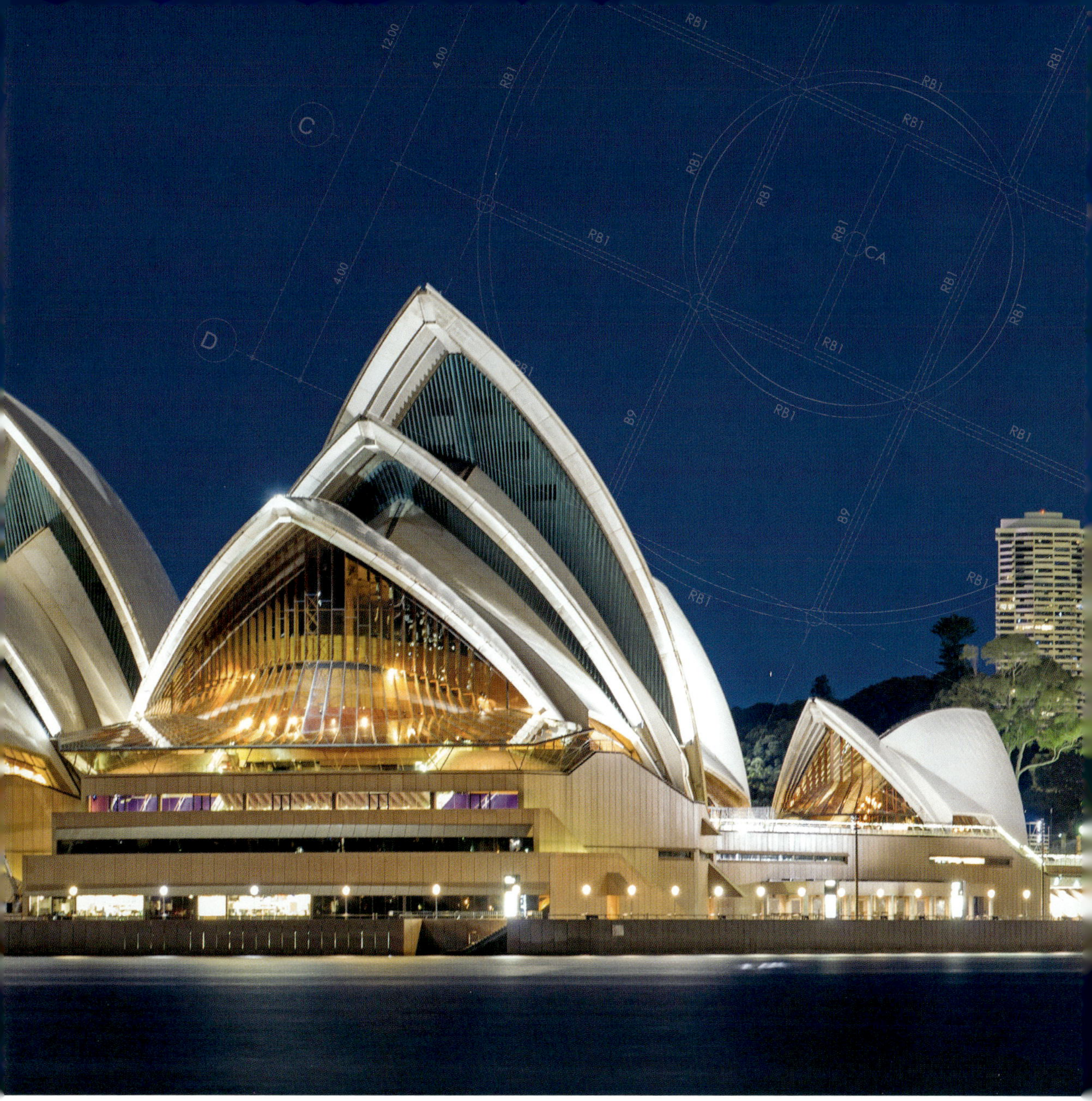

FACT BOX

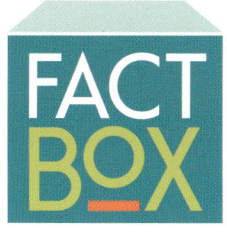

An architect is a person who designs buildings. Architecture is the art of designing buildings.

To design and **engineer** such a cutting-edge building was not easy. For years, Utzon worked with a large team of architects and engineers to finalize the plans for the building. One of the biggest **obstacles** was figuring out how to create the concrete shells that would form the roof. Eventually, Utzon came up with what he called the "spherical solution" to build the shell-shaped roof. It was based on the idea of breaking a sphere into parts and using those parts in a new and different way. Then he and his team used math and geometry to come up with the precise shapes and measurements for the roof. It was an exciting union of engineering and design.

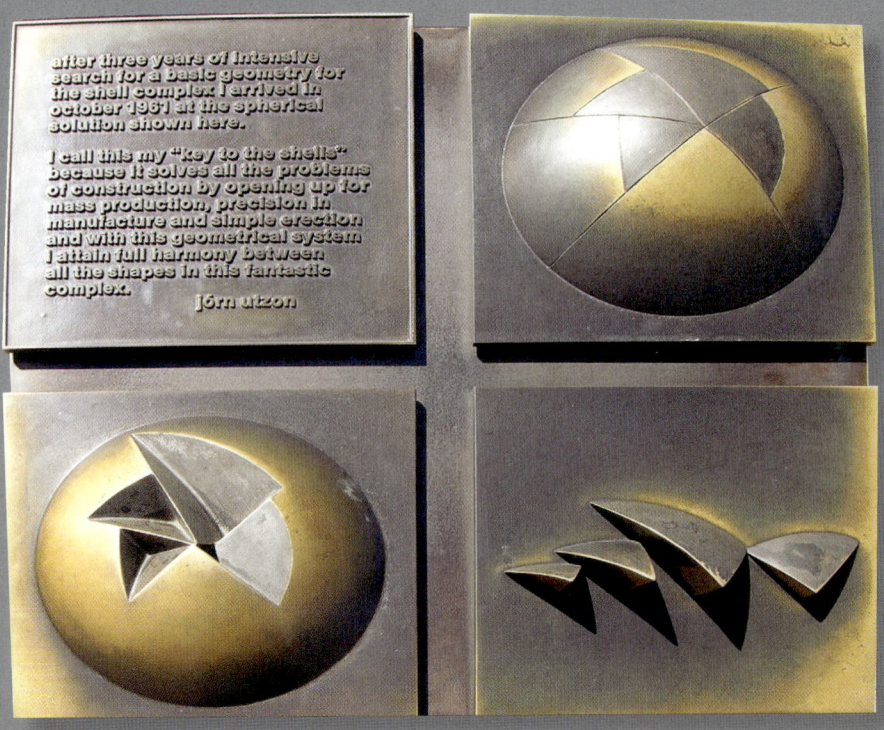

Utzon's spherical solution

In March 1959, the construction of the Sydney Opera House began. The structure was built in three stages. During the first stage, the **podium** where the building sits would be constructed. After that, the roof shells would be built and covered with shiny white tiles. The interior would be completed last.

Jørn Utzon in front of the Sydney Opera House in 1965

Utzon called the spherical solution "the key to the shells." He said, "It solves all the problems of construction." And with it, he could "reach full **harmony** between all the shapes in this fantastic complex."

However, in 1966, midway through the Sydney Opera House's construction, the Australian government questioned Utzon's work. They worried that the opera house was taking too long and becoming too expensive to build. They hired an architect named Peter Hall to take over and complete the building, which he did in 1973.

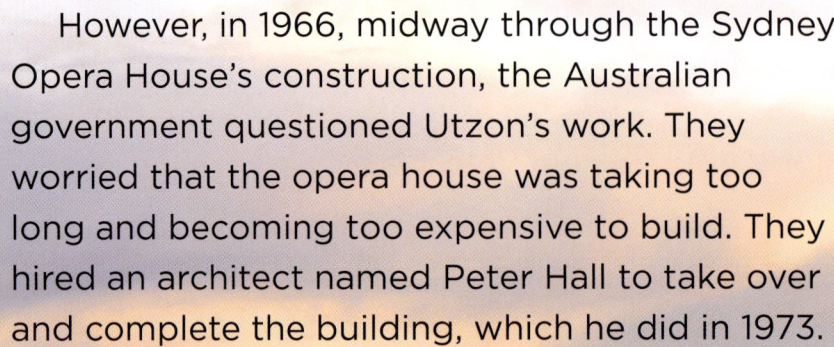

FACT BOX

Not everyone liked the Sydney Opera House. Fellow modern architect Frank Lloyd Wright said, "This circus tent is not architecture."

When the Sydney Opera House was finally finished, people from around the world marveled at it. Many called it a modern masterpiece. While Utzon was disappointed that he wasn't able to complete his project, he was proud of his vision. "To me it is a great joy to know how much the building is loved," said Utzon. In 2007, the Sydney Opera House was recognized as one of the most outstanding places on Earth on the **UNESCO** World Heritage List.

What Is Modern Architecture?

Look around. Buildings are everywhere. All buildings are created using architecture, a combination of science and art. Architects use different elements to express their vision for a building. For example, they consider the shape, size, material, color, and other factors. However, architects are not like sculptors who create artworks purely for their own sake. Architecture has an important purpose, which is to create a physical place for people. One of an architect's main jobs is to figure out how a building will be used and who will use it. For example, an airport is vastly different from a museum or church. And a house functions differently than a hospital or a bank.

After architects come up with an idea for a building and before the building is constructed, they sketch out plans. The plans map out the building's interior and exterior, including the materials to be used.

Throughout history, there have been various styles of architecture. Some buildings are grand and impressive, while others are plain and **unadorned**. Each style is a reflection of the architect and the needs and desires of the people who use the buildings.

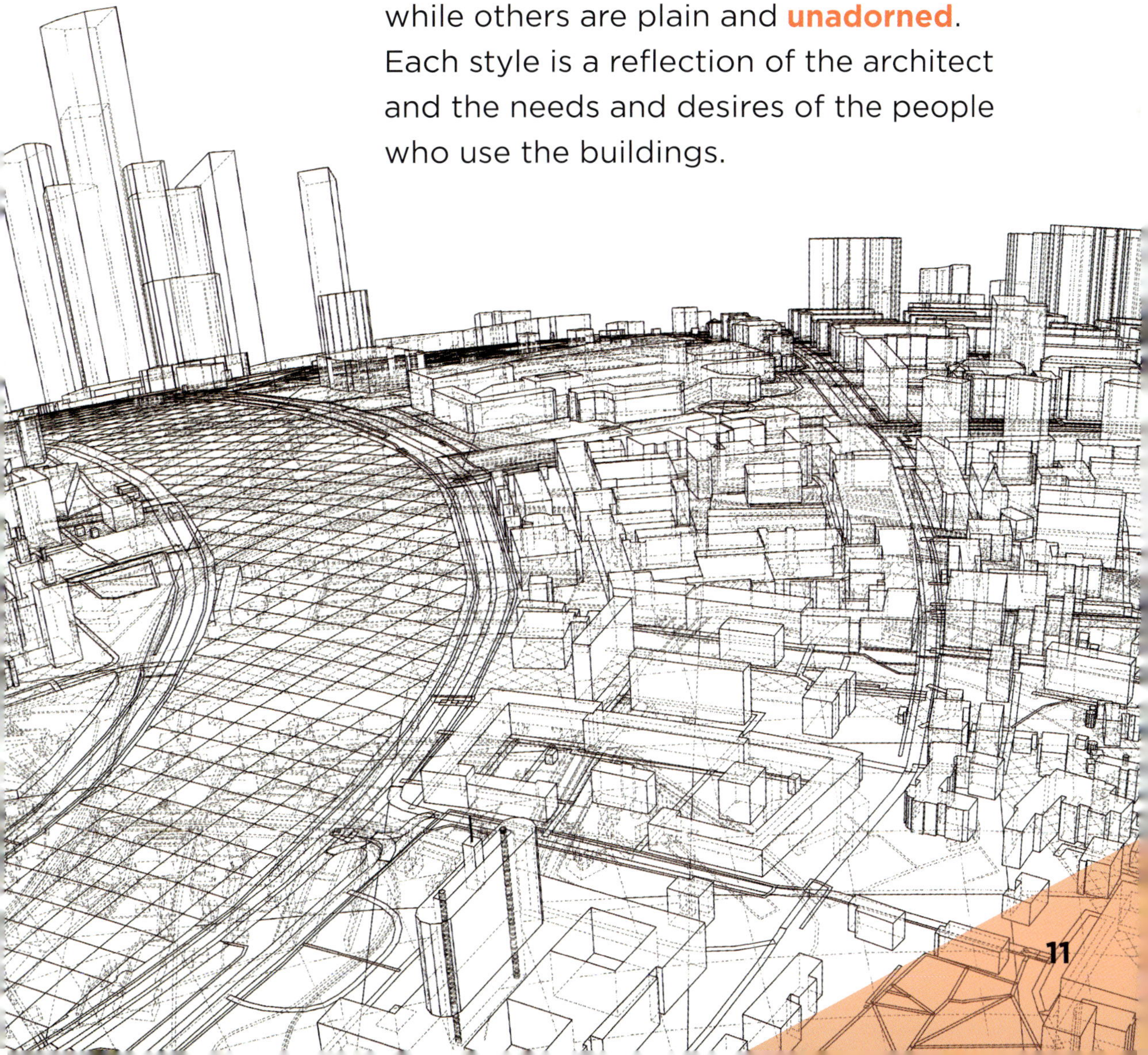

Modern architecture is one of dozens of styles of architecture. It developed in the late 1800s when more people moved to cities. As they did, the **population** of cities grew and land became scarcer. Architects took notice and began building tall buildings that could hold more people on smaller parcels of land. This led to the construction of skyscrapers! At the time, bricks were often used to construct buildings. However, bricks couldn't support very tall buildings. In 1885, an architect named William Le Baron Jenney designed a strong internal steel frame to support the very first skyscraper.

The steel-framed Flatiron Building in New York City is an early skyscraper. It got its name because it resembles an old-fashioned clothing iron!

One of the most famous skyscraper architects was Louis Sullivan. He strongly believed that a building's exterior design should reflect its interior function. In other words, Sullivan thought function should be the starting point for a building's design. He famously said, "Form follows function." Frank Lloyd Wright, who worked for Sullivan, disagreed. He said, "Form and function should be one." The idea of modern architecture is based on these principles.

Frank Lloyd Wright

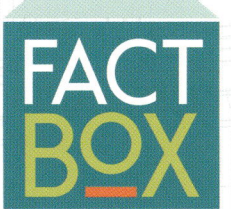

Frank Lloyd Wright (1867–1959) was an American architect who designed private homes as well as public buildings.

Building Modern

Modern architecture became widespread around World War II (1939–1945). That's when many architects started rejecting what they thought were too many details and decorations on buildings. Instead, they embraced clean, simple lines and forms, which is known as minimalism. They also wanted to use the newest **technology** and building materials that included steel, glass, and concrete. These architects believed that building materials should be on display rather than tucked away where people can't see them.

Victorian architecture was popular from 1830 to around 1910. This style emphasized height, various shapes and colors, and lots of decoration.

14

There were many **pioneers** of modern architecture. Their buildings shaped what we recognize today as this style. One of the most influential was Frank Lloyd Wright. Even though he said he hated modern buildings, Wright was a key figure in the movement. And many of his buildings are defining examples of the style.

This is an example of modern architecture, showcasing boxy shapes, clean lines, and little decoration.

Frank Lloyd Wright was born in Wisconsin in 1867 and studied engineering in college. In 1893, he started his own architecture firm. Nature was Wright's biggest influence. He once said, "Stay close to nature. It will never fail you." Wright brought natural elements, such as light and water, into his designs. He thought of his buildings as a whole where form and function worked together. To him, the best architecture considered location, including the landscape and **climate**, in addition to structure, function, and building materials.

Wright used modern construction materials such as concrete, glass, and steel. He created flat concrete roofs—a signature of modern style—on many of the homes and buildings he designed. One of his best-known modern houses is Fallingwater, which was a family's vacation home. It is perched above a waterfall in a forest. The house is made from giant slabs of concrete, along with sandstone, steel, and glass. He matched the color of the concrete to the back of a fallen leaf found on the property. Much of the sandstone used for the house came from the surrounding land. Wright's Fallingwater beautifully blended nature and design.

Fallingwater is located in Mill Run, Pennsylvania. The house was completed in 1939.

Wright famously said of his architecture, "The whole is [to] the part, what the part is to the whole."

17

The Guggenheim was the only museum Wright ever designed. It opened in 1959.

Wright's most **iconic** modern building is New York City's Guggenheim Museum. The museum has a **cylinder** shape that's wider at the top. Inside is a continuous spiraling ramp that ends under a huge skylight. It's thought that the ramp was inspired by the spiral-shaped interior of a nautilus shell.

And Wright might have been thinking about a spider's web when he designed the skylight. However, many of the building's shapes were based on geometry and **abstract** ideas. "These geometric forms suggest human ideas, moods, and **sentiments**," Wright said about his building. Before the museum opened, people criticized its design. How could art be hung on the curved walls? They also wondered if the architecture would **overshadow** the art. "On the contrary," Wright replied. The design makes "the building and the painting an uninterrupted, beautiful **symphony** such as never existed in the world of art before."

The museum's spiraling ramp and skylight

19

Le Corbusier's birth name was Charles-Édouard Jeanneret-Gris. But he renamed himself *Le Corbusier*, which means "the crow-like one" in French. He was also a painter and sculptor.

Another important modern architect was a Swiss man named Le Corbusier. Born in 1887, Le Corbusier was mostly self-taught. In 1923, he wrote a 200-page book about architecture, which is still used by architects today. Le Corbusier started designing and constructing buildings in the early 1900s and worked for 5 decades. "Everything is sky and light, space and simplicity," he once said. He dreamed up houses made from white concrete cubes and skyscrapers covered with gardens.

In 1929, Le Corbusier designed a family home called Villa Savoye. It has a sleek, white exterior, flat roof, and long windows. Large concrete pillars raise the house off the ground. Le Corbusier also designed the furniture for the home. The architect proudly called his work "a machine for living." Many critics raved about it as a great modern achievement. Others were less sure, including the family who lived there. They moved out in 1936 after the roof constantly leaked.

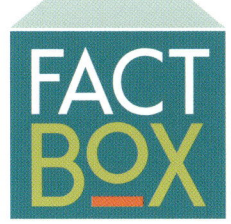

Le Corbusier didn't work alone. One of his partners was a woman architect and furniture designer named Charlotte Perriand. Unfortunately, she received little credit for her contributions.

Villa Savoye is located near Paris, France. It's now a museum.

Other Key Examples

More **quintessential** modern buildings were designed in the late 1940s and early 1950s. In addition to Wright and Le Corbusier, Ludwig Mies van der Rohe was a leading modern architect. Born in Germany, he spent years working in the United States. His bold designs included a lot of metal and glass. From 1946 to 1951, Mies designed and built the Farnsworth House for Dr. Edith Farnsworth near Chicago, Illinois. The building has a concrete floor, a steel frame, and floor-to-ceiling glass windows. The windows bring nature inside and allow light to flood the main living space, which has few walls. Mies called his style "skin and bones" architecture. He also coined the phrase, "Less is more"—a saying that is still used to describe modern architecture.

Ludwig Mies van der Rohe

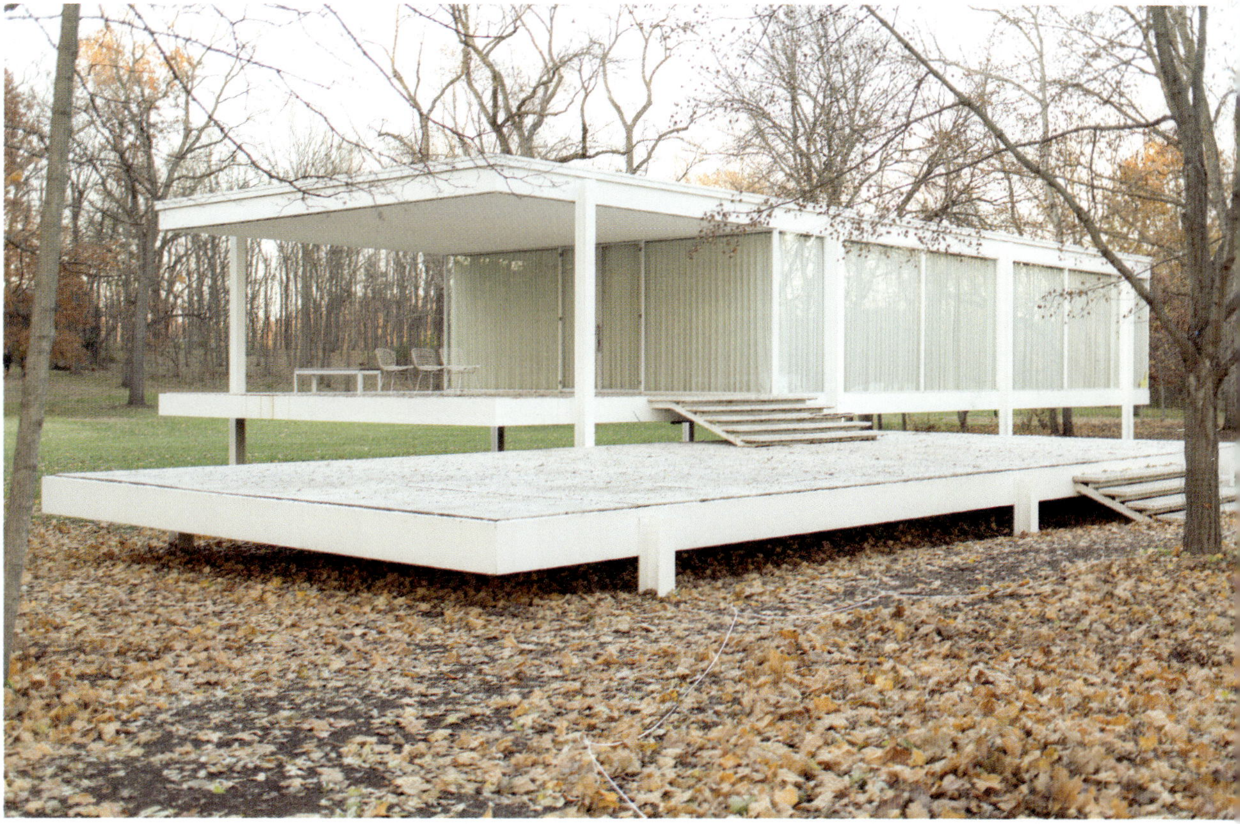

Dr. Farnsworth deeply disliked her new house and claimed it was not fit for a person to live in.

FACT BOX

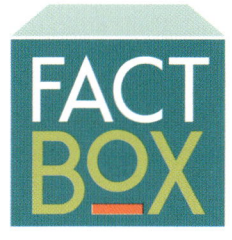

Ludwig Mies van der Rohe was a leader of what's called the Bauhaus school of design in Germany. Many office buildings were built in this style.

Philip Johnson's Glass House in Connecticut

Mies's work had a big impact on American architect Philip Johnson. In fact, Johnson designed a version of a glass house for himself in 1949! Johnson's building, though, was different from Mies's. Instead of stark white, he chose dark colors. He also used wood and brick accents. As a result, the house felt warmer and more grounded. Johnson built variations of his glass houses for many years. He also designed much larger structures.

In 1956, Mies and Johnson **collaborated** to build the Seagram Building, a 39-story skyscraper. The partnership resulted in a sleek, elegant bronze and glass tower. It was one of the first office buildings of its kind to use these materials. The Seagram Building was so admired that it became one of the "most copied buildings" in the world.

The Seagram Building in New York City

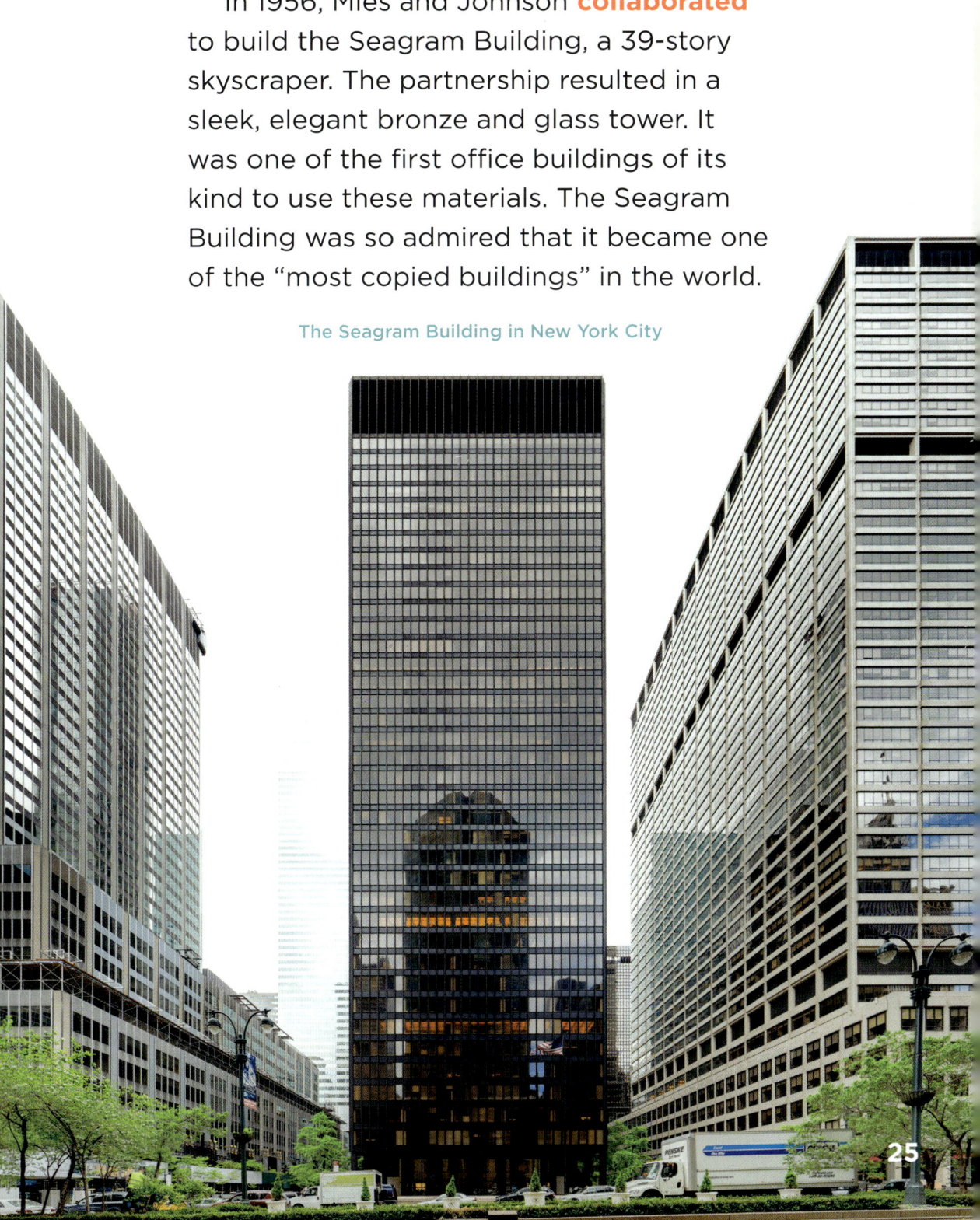

After Modernism

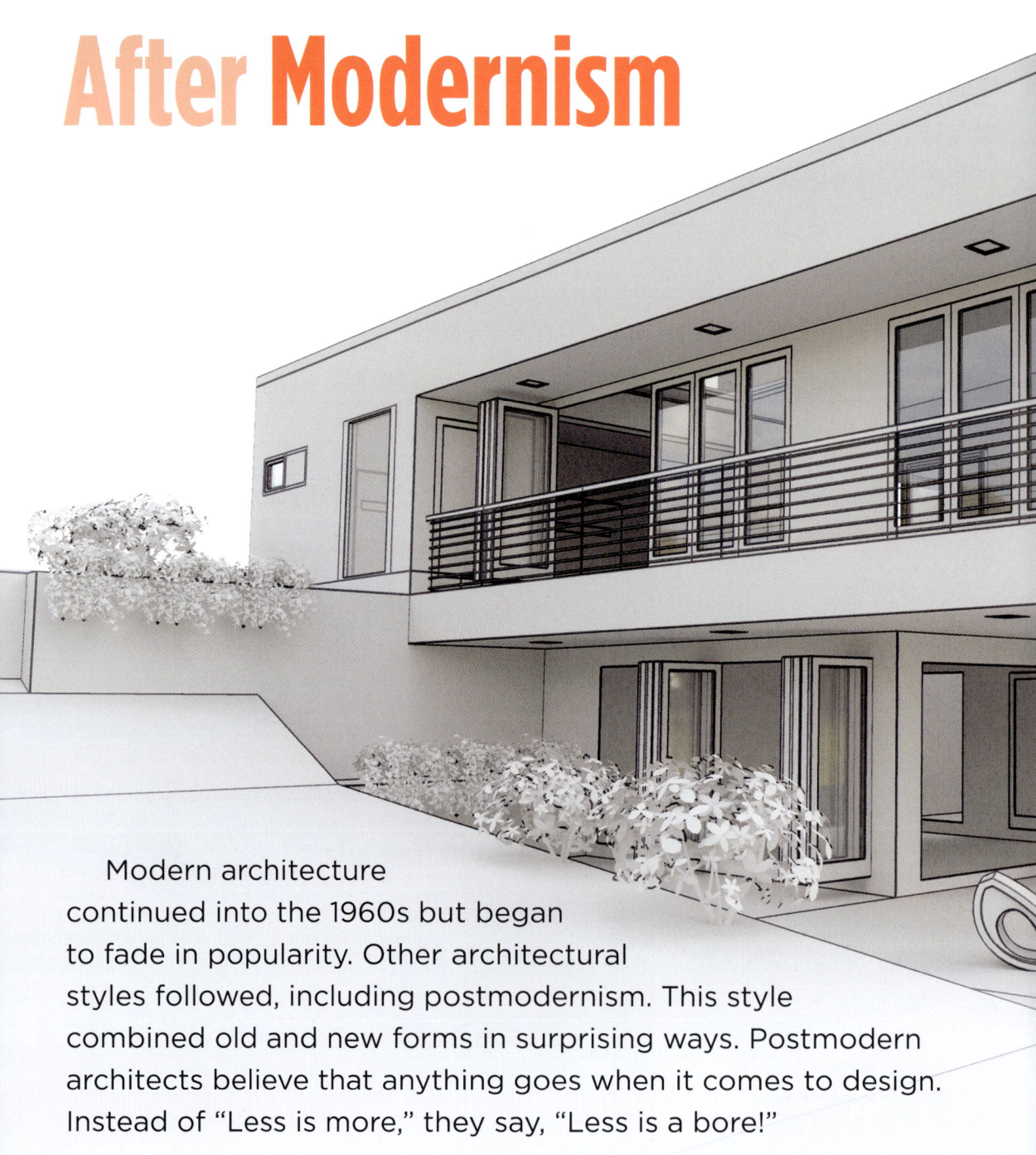

Modern architecture continued into the 1960s but began to fade in popularity. Other architectural styles followed, including postmodernism. This style combined old and new forms in surprising ways. Postmodern architects believe that anything goes when it comes to design. Instead of "Less is more," they say, "Less is a bore!"

Postmodernism was also a reaction to what critics believed were shortcomings of modern architecture. For example, the flat roofs of many modern buildings badly leaked. The steel rusted. Some buildings, like Wright's Fallingwater, had significant structural issues. Despite these issues, modern architecture never fully disappeared. It continues to have a strong influence on architecture today. The next time you go outside, see what modern architecture you can find!

FACT BOX

The word *post* means "after" or "subsequent" to. So *postmodernism* means "after modernism."

Design a Modern Building

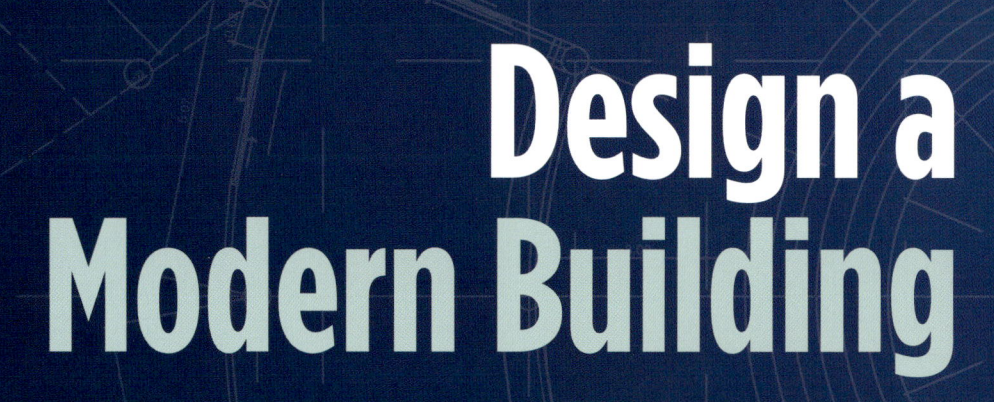

Think about what you just learned about modern architecture in this book. Now use that information to design your own modern building!

DESIGN CONCEPT: What is your idea for your building? Where will it be located? What will it be used for? What materials will you use to build it? Consider your building's form *and* function.

PLAN: Think about what the exterior and interior of your building will look like. How will people move around and through your building? How will it fit into the landscape? How big or small will it be?

DRAW: Grab some paper and a pencil. Sketch the floor plan of your building to show the arrangement of rooms. Label each room. Make sure to include doorways and windows! Next, draw an **elevation** plan that shows the exterior, sides, and height of the building, noting what materials will be used.

BUILD A MODEL: Use materials around your home, such as paper, cardboard, scissors, straws, popsicle sticks, and glue, to build a small model of your building.

REFINE YOUR PLAN: What works about your design? What doesn't work? Make any needed changes to improve your building.

GLOSSARY

abstract (ab-STRAKT) existing as a thought or idea; not based on a particular thing

climate (KLYE-mit) patterns of weather over a long period of time

collaborated (kuh-LAB-uh-reyt-uhd) worked together

cylinder (SIL-in-der) a circular solid shape with parallel sides

elevation (el-uh-VAY-shun) a particular side of a building

engineer (en-jun-NIHR) to design and build something

harmony (HAHR-muh-nee) the state of forming a pleasing whole

modern (MOD-urn) a style that is marked by a shift from traditions

obstacles (OB-stuh-kulz) things that slow down progress

overshadow (oh-ver-SHAD-oh) to be more significant than something else

pioneers (pye-uh-NEERZ) the first people to do something

podium (POH-dee-uhm) a platform

population (pop-yuh-LAY-shuhn) the total number of people living in a place

quintessential (kwin-tuh-SEN-shuhl) the essence of something

sentiments (SEN-tuh-muhnts) attitudes toward something

symphony (SIM-fuh-nee) a pleasing combination

technology (tek-NOL-uh-jee) the science of making useful things

temples (TEM-puhlz) buildings where people worship

unadorned (un-UH-dawrned) not decorated; plain

UNESCO (yoo-NES-koh) the United Nations Educational, Scientific, and Cultural Organization; an agency of the United Nations that encourages the exchange of ideas, information, and culture

READ MORE

Allen, Peter. *Atlas of Amazing Architecture*. London: Cicada Books, 2021.

Armstrong, Simon. *Cool Architecture*. London: Pavilion, 2015.

Dillon, Patrick. *The Story of Buildings*. Somerville, MA: Candlewick Press, 2014.

Glancey, Jonathan. *Architecture: A Visual History*. London: DK, 2021.

Moreno, Mark. *Architecture for Kids*. Emeryville, VA: Rockridge Press, 2021.

LEARN MORE ONLINE

Architecture for Children
https://archforkids.com

Britannica Kids: Architecture
https://kids.britannica.com/students/article/architecture/272939

Center for Architecture: Architecture at Home Resources
https://www.centerforarchitecture.org/k-12/resources/

Lego Design Challenge
https://www.architects.org/uploads/BSA_LWW_LEGO_Challenge.pdf

STEAM Exercises: Kid Architecture
http://www.vancebm.com/kidArchitect/pages/steamExercises.html

INDEX

architects, 4–6, 8, 10, 12–14, 20–22, 24, 26
Bauhaus school of design, 23
building materials, 11, 14, 16–17, 25, 29
building use, 10–11
concrete, 6, 14, 17, 20–21
Fallingwater, 17, 27
Farnsworth House, 22–23
Flatiron Building, 12–13
geometry, 6, 19
glass, 14, 17, 22, 24
Guggenheim Museum (New York), 18
Hall, Peter, 8
Jenney, William Le Baron, 12
Johnson, Philip, 24–25
Le Corbusier, 20–21
math, 6
Mies van der Rohe, Ludwig, 22–25
minimalism, 14
modern architecture
 defining, 10–11
 designing your own, 28–29
 shortcomings of, 27
nature, 16–17
Perriand, Charlotte, 21
postmodernism, 26–27
Seagram Building, 25
sketches, 11
skyscrapers, 12
spherical construction, 6–7
steel, 12, 14, 17
Sullivan, Louis, 13
Sydney Opera House, 4–9
technology, 14
UNESCO World Heritage List, 9
Utzon, Jørn, 4–9
Victorian architecture, 14
Villa Savoye, 21
World War II, 14
Wright, Frank Lloyd, 8, 13, 15–19

ABOUT THE AUTHOR

Joyce Markovics has written hundreds of books for young readers. She lives in a nearly 200-year-old carpenter Gothic style house along the Hudson River. Joyce would like to thank architect, designer, and city planner Jeff Shumaker for his insight and help creating this series. She dedicates this book to Jason Feldman, a dear friend with a refined eye.